# GETTING BACK YOUR FOCUS.

## Regaining your attention and fostering deep thought.

By

## Hank G. Minton

# Copyright

All rights reserved. No part of this publication may be reproduced, distributed, or transmitted in any form or by any means, including photocopying, recording, or other electronic or mechanical methods, without the prior written permission of the publisher, except as permitted by copyright law.

# Table of contents.

# INTRODUCTION

The capacity to retain constant attention has become a valuable and elusive skill in the modern world, where distractions are common and information overload is the norm. The continual barrage of alerts, the never-ending stream of emails, and the siren melody of social media all compete for our attention in the era we live in. It's understandable that our capacity to focus intently and deliberately has decreased in this chaotic atmosphere. You need not worry, however, since this book, "Getting Back Your Focus," will show you how to recapture the power of concentration and unleash your entire cognitive potential. The concepts and techniques in these pages are designed to help you achieve, whether you're a student trying to thrive in your academics, a professional trying to increase productivity, or just someone looking for a more thoughtful and meaningful existence. The chapters that follow will take you on a tour through the complexities of attention, the intriguing operations of the human brain, and the disclosure of useful methods for improving your concentration. We'll examine the psychology of distraction, analyze the mental conflicts being fought by your brain, and provide you with a toolkit of tried-and-true techniques to recapture your lost concentration. The difficulties presented by this "age of distraction" are actual, but so are the possibilities for overcoming them. "Getting Back Your Focus" provides a strategy for prevailing in the conflict for your attention. It's an invitation to rediscover the thrill of deep thinking, to reconnect with the joys of continuous focus, and to recover the precious moments of your life from the grips of distraction. As you set out on this path, keep in mind that the capacity for concentration is a talent that can be fostered and improved rather than a fixed attribute. With perseverance, comprehension, and the appropriate techniques, you may regain a state of sharpened focus and benefit from the transforming influence it has on all facets of your life. Together, let's go out on this adventure and explore the tremendous benefits of "Getting Back Your Focus."

# Chapter 1

## **The Era of Distraction**.

The current period is referred to as the "age of distraction" since technology and numerous media have permeated our everyday lives, increasing degrees of distraction and shortening attention spans. With the introduction of cellphones, social media platforms, and continual connectivity, it is getting harder and harder for people to concentrate on their work and have uninterrupted, in-depth thought processes.

The proliferation of cellphones is one of the primary causes of distraction. We now rely heavily on these gadgets since they give us rapid access to information, communication, and entertainment. With notifications, texts, and social media updates competing for our attention all the time, they also operate as persistent sources of distraction. Studies have demonstrated that even when a smartphone is not in use, its sheer presence may have a major negative impact on cognition and attention.

Another important element in the age of distraction is social media platforms. In order to keep users interested for a long time, platforms like Facebook, Twitter, and Instagram have included features like unlimited scrolling and tailored content streams. A sensation of FOMO (fear of missing out) and a desire for regular validation are brought on by the constant flood of updates, likes, and comments, which furthers distraction and lowers productivity.

 The sheer amount of information at our disposal is another factor contributing to the era of distraction, along with cellphones and social media. The internet has made it very simple to acquire a wide variety of information, but it has also made it challenging to cut through the clutter and concentrate on what is most important. It might be difficult to focus on one thing at a time due to information overload caused by the continual barrage of news, articles, videos, and advertising.

Our attention spans have also been significantly impacted by the age of distraction. Our capacity for sustained attention and in-depth, concentrated thought has decreased with time, according to research. This might not be good for our jobs, relationships, or general wellbeing. It has been harder to participate in tasks that demand sustained focus and mental effort in a society where multitasking is praised and continual stimulation is the norm.

It's crucial to remember that not all forms of diversion are detrimental. Some types of diversion, including taking quick breaks or participating in leisure pursuits, can actually boost creativity and productivity. Finding a balance and creating effective distraction management techniques are crucial.

People can use a variety of tactics to counteract the age of distraction. These consist of:

1. Establishing boundaries: designating time slots for uninterrupted, concentrated work or recreational activities.
2. Mindfulness practice: using mindfulness practices to increase focus and lessen the influence of distractions, such as deep breathing exercises or meditation.
3. Establishing designated times or places when cellphones and other gadgets are prohibited, such as before bed or during meals,making use of productivity tools,

such as software or applications that may block distracting websites or set time limits for particular tasks.

4. Setting task priorities: deciding which tasks are most crucial to do first in order to give them the focus they require.

5. Doing intense work: setting aside time specifically for intense, uninterrupted work that necessitates continued focus and mental exertion.

6. Using single-tasking techniques: concentrating on one activity at a time and refraining from multitasking, which can reduce productivity and increase distractions.

# Chapter 2.

## Understanding attention in the digital age.

The currency of the digital era is attention. How we spend our time in a world where we are always inundated with information affects how we live our lives.

It's no secret that online businesses profit from the amount of time users spend on their platform, which promotes highly efficient and incentive-driven digital interactions.

These expertly crafted goods have made it difficult for us to maintain attention control. Not us, but the deceptive tactics encouraged by profit-driven institutions are to blame. Facebook generated $22 billion in revenue in 2018, with an average daily use time of 43 minutes. Time is indeed money.

I was previously a victim of these attention-grabbing tactics. I kept track of how much time I spent on screens and discovered that I spent 2 hours every day on social media, which added up to 4 hours of phone usage. That struck me as absurd, which ignited a fire inside of me to alter how I value my attention and boost my productivity.

Over the past few months, I've done research, tried things out, and done things. I now only use my phone for 1-2 hours total each day, which is a significant improvement. (And those hours generally entail useful work like direct communication.)

I'll go more deeply into the reasons behind our attention deficit in this  chapter and offer my findings and strategies. I hope my experiences might be helpful to you.

- **The importance of attention**.

Shallow and deep attention are the two primary categories. Reading an email, replying to a text, or touching a notification are all examples of activities that require very little effort but nevertheless constitute shallow attention. On the other hand, paying attention deeply demands significant effort. It's the labor we put in to produce something meaningful, such as a budget for our own use or a piece of art.

- **Opportunity cost.**

Opportunity cost or the rewards you give up when selecting one option over another, is a fundamental concept in economics. There is an opportunity cost to everything you do.

 The opportunity cost is a loss of depth when we interrupt an activity that demands intense concentration to check social media or email instead. We temporarily feel satisfied by completing the shallow task, but we forfeit the concentration we had previously committed to the crucial task.

 We thrive in depth. When we are deeply joyful, it lasts for a long time and motivates us to persevere in the face of difficulty. Instead of being constantly interrupted by a barrage of uninteresting chores, our brain is free to concentrate and appreciate the current work.

Long-term, focused effort propels us to develop and introduce fresh concepts since it's the only way we can produce anything of real value.

Time Spent * Intensity of Focus = Quality of Work

This equation demonstrates that, given a fixed amount of time, the quality of the work we create depends on our concentration (i.e., how well we use our attention).

As a result, we should concentrate on the current activity, control distractions (shallow tasks), and let ourselves get lost in the excitement and difficulty of deep labor.

Apps were made to hook us. The main concern while creating Facebook, according to Sean Parker, the company's founding president, "was how to consume as much of your time and conscious attention as possible."

Three key psychological techniques are used by Facebook and other applications to keep you hooked: validation, variable reward, and innate curiosity.

**Validation**:

According to Maslow's hierarchy of needs, everyone wants to be validated by others. Many of the tiny and big decisions we make every day in today's world are motivated by this need for approval.

Our brains seek rapid approval, which apps offer in a way that isn't always possible in the real world. The "likes," "reactions," and "comments" you get in response to social media posts serve as a type of affirmation. Receiving a few makes you feel unimportant and unnoticed, but receiving many makes you feel amazing and appreciated.

The affirmation we receive feeds the loop, increasing our attentional investment in the app.

**Varying reward**:

Operant conditioning was developed in the 1930s by B.F. Skinner became popular with the discovery of the potent effects of varied reinforcement. In essence, incentives are given out following a variable number of acts or times, resulting in a very high, consistent rate of response.

Social media carries forth this concept by distributing engaging and private posts around your stream (while also including information that makes money)

distributing notifications that appear to be random for non-user interactions (such as birthdays, group activities, X buddy likes Y, etc.).

Various triggers throughout the day (someone "going live," "missed posts," "trending," etc.) cause the prompting app to appear.

Our brains are trained to use applications in quest of little rewards due to the diversity and endless scroll (the opportunity to keep looking for rewards).

**Innate Curiosity:**

Humans are incredibly inquisitive creatures. We are pushed to be "in the loop" with news about the people near us and to learn what we don't know.

 By enabling continual connectivity, apps serve to worsen this concept. In order to ensure that we never miss out on any information, we spend more time than is necessary on platforms.

There are several techniques to reduce interruptions and maintain concentration on difficult work. I'll list my top 7 strategies that, throughout the years, have proven effective for me in the hopes that they may also be helpful to you.

- **Disable Notifications**.

The most common type of distraction is a notification. These "calls to action" are only brief assignments. My alerts are only sent to those who need to get in touch with me. All we have are phone calls and texts.

- **Reflect.**

You must teach your brain to focus for extended periods of time if you want to immerse yourself in important work. While meditation often focuses on not paying attention to anything in particular, it also helps you become used to having times without interruption. I've found that getting your thoughts clean before bed takes around three to five minutes.

- **Use your finest mental work time to play**.

Determine the time of day when you are cognitively most effective. At this point, set aside a significant amount of time for deep work. When you feel the most concentrated (typically just before or after lunch), you'll recognize it. Make the most of your peak hours since not all hours of the day are created equal.

- **Take breaks when you need them.**

If you are unable to give a profound task all your mental effort, it is meaningless. Take pauses when you need to refresh. After 1-2 hours of work, I've found that 10-15 minute breaks are ideal. But instead of going into the "check my phone" mentality, get a sip of water, go for a stroll, or chat with a coworker. Look for activities that are deeper tasks.

- **Schedule your email checks (avoid switching tasks).**

It's simple to constantly monitor and respond to emails. But most email correspondence consists of brief chores. Plan when you're going to check your email; depending on how busy I am, I try to do it 3–6 times a day. This recommendation is more adaptable because some tasks and vocations do necessitate continuous communication.

- **Disconnect**.

Email advertisements may be grating. To free up space in your inbox and save the mental strain of having to read them, unsubscribe from any email chains that aren't linked to your job.

- **Minimize checking social media.**

Since social media has benefits and may be enjoyable, I do not support quitting it altogether. I instead set a daily cap of three social media checks. Knowing when I'm going to participate makes it easier for me to control my natural curiosity because I know I'll ultimately view all the posts.

# Chapter 3.

## The Brain and Its Struggle for Focus.

The capacity for concentration is among the most crucial abilities for learning. You would be able to learn more information more rapidly if you could concentrate your attention on a single job for extended periods of time.

But it's difficult to focus. Part of the explanation is that we are unable to control distractions. Focus, information overload, and the drawbacks of multitasking are topics I've written about in the past, but this is a vast and intriguing topic.

**The mental battle.**

Attention, which is something of an unseen force but which, as we have discovered before, may help us understand the previously unknown, plays a significant role in improving focus. For instance, the majority of us will have a map of our brain's most frequently visited locations, known as a priority map. Its importance comes from the fact that it may be utilized to determine how we rank incoming information and, consequently, where we focus our attention. It is vital to note that while attention is a finite resource, how we use it matters.

Find out just how attentive you are by taking this test.

The issue is that these maps alter according to how "relevant" the data is, and relevance depends on three systems that are always in conflict with one another. I realize that this is becoming more difficult, but persevere and pay attention!

- **The administrative system**

This system, which is the principal one and is located in the frontal lobe, directs attention in accordance with our present objectives. For instance, I will turn to page 4 and begin reading since I need to learn about double-entry bookkeeping.

- **The system of rewards**.

This is the system that rewards us, as you might expect. The dopamine surge you experience while checking your smartphone might be a reward, but you should actually be reading page 4! Additionally, it is made worse by the fact that the brain's focus is drawn to flashing lights, which frequently occur when a text message arrives.

- **The habit system:**

This uses set norms that are frequently formed over time by repetition. Perhaps this is why you keep checking your phone to see if you've received a text message even when you know you haven't since you would have noticed the flashing light. These systems are vying for your attention, hence the name "war in the brain."

**How to focus more effectively.**

Although there is no miraculous cure and some of the ways below will seem apparent, I hope you will be more willing to try them because there is a scientific basis for why they might help.

- **Reduce distractions.**

If checking your phone requires a lot of work, the benefit you receive from doing so will be lessened. The best advice is to avoid using your phone or anything else that can divert your attention when you're studying. Have a study area that is calm, uncomplicated, and free from anything fascinating that may be a distraction. Finally, even if there is conflicting research about the benefits of background music or white noise, it would be worthwhile to give it a shot.

- **Set objectives to help your executive system.**

Be sure to write them down and keep them from being overly ambitious.

It's difficult to concentrate while you're experiencing high amounts of anxiety, so quiet down and relax. There are a number of techniques to aid with relaxing, such as deep breathing (see this video; it's quite useful) and, of course, exercise, which I have previously talked about because it is a natural stress reliever.

- **Avoid excessive stimulation.**

Since it might cause your reward system to get ingrained with novelty-seeking behaviors like playing video games. They might give the impression that studying is highly tedious and unsatisfying, especially if you just finished playing a game. Hold onto it until later, possibly as a treat.

# Chapter 4.

# Breaking Free from Multitasking Madness.

### Why do people multitask?

The practice of handling several things at once is referred to as multitasking. Multitasking is a typical tactic used by professionals to boost their effectiveness and productivity at work. For instance, some professionals might think that reading emails over lunch or holding a phone call while driving can help them do their tasks more quickly.

Contrary to popular assumption, real multitasking is rather uncommon, and the majority of professionals who engage in it on a regular basis actually transition between activities rather than completing them all at once. As a result, multitasking has a number of drawbacks relating to attention deficiency, memory, and distractibility. When deciding how to best utilize their skills, professionals may find it advantageous to take into account these drawbacks and other efficiency options.

**Are humans capable of multitasking?**

No and yes.
Our brains are capable of doing many things at once. We can, for instance, breathe while walking. The automatic, neurological activities will be eliminated from the discussion for the

remainder of this essay, which will instead concentrate on conscious, voluntary behaviors (such as eating at the movies, texting while having a conversation, etc.).

The problem arises when we attempt to carry out many conscious tasks that call for equal attention. Even though it might result in overeating, weight gain, etc., this may not be a problem when it comes to a movie or snack, but it can cause issues when it comes to critical work.

**What risks do multitaskers face?**
Professionals may take into account the numerous risks linked with multitasking while using it at work. To better comprehend the effects of multitasking on productivity, aptitude, and health, the following hazards are described:

- **Miscommunication.**

Communication already leaves a lot open to interpretation. It is a recipe for disaster and can result in misunderstandings when we undertake another action that takes concentration (such as listening while sending a text message that has nothing to do with what we are hearing).

Avoid using your cellphone during conversations (particularly in meetings), as doing so is disrespectful and prevents your brain from fully processing what is being said. You also run the risk of sending erroneous SMS.

- **Stress and confidence concerns**.

When we have inflated notions of our abilities, we may feel let down by ourselves and become more stressed. The cultural expectations in South Asia are already very high; we frequently live in a world of continual comparison with regard to things like marriage, motherhood, wealth, and education. Although both sexes are subject to high demands, South Asian women may be forced to balance both modern expectations and traditional cultural ones (such as being a wife who cooks fresh meals every day while simultaneously working).

- **Ineffectiveness and decreased productivity**

Professionals that regularly move between jobs rather than finishing each one at a time may take longer to accomplish their work as a result of multitasking. Therefore, multitasking might result in ineffective time management. Professionals may then encounter issues relating to lost productivity.

- **Possible errors**.

Professionals who multitask must divide their focus between multiple tasks. When focused on one task at a time, this might cause professionals to make mistakes that they might not otherwise make as they carry out their tasks. Over time, these errors can force experts to verify their work thoroughly, which could result in inefficiencies and a general loss of productivity.

- **Lack of imagination**

Multitasking frequently requires a significant percentage of working memory for professionals. This may sap their motivation and limit their ability to think creatively. As a result, multitasking may affect a professional's capacity for innovative problem-solving, analysis of complicated problems, and problem-solving.

- **Memory problems.**

Professionals frequently overlook crucial information when multitasking. A further risk is that trying to multitask may interfere with short-term memory. As a result, multitasking may impair a professional's memory for specifics of their job and ability to resume duties productively following pauses.

People who multitask regularly usually have a hard time deciding which disruptions are important enough to pay attention to. This may make it more likely for a professional to become sidetracked by inconsequential interruptions like email notifications, text messages, and conversations among coworkers. From here, such experts can find it difficult to maintain concentration on their work for an extended period of time and finish their assignments on schedule.

- **Mental health and persistent stress.**

Regular multitaskers may be more susceptible to chronic stress because they are constantly exposed to tasks that divert their attention. Furthermore, multitasking can have an adverse effect on a professional's mental health since it increases the risk of error, extends the time needed to complete a task, and reduces creativity. As a result, multitasking may make professionals more likely than their non-multitasking colleagues to experience poor self-esteem, anxiety, and despair.

## Effective methods for escaping the chaos of multitasking

### 1. Prioritize your tasks.

To prioritize your duties, decide which ones are the most crucial or urgent and give them top priority.

You can make sure that you are spending your time and resources wisely and that the most important activities are finished first by setting priorities for your workload.

Making a note of every activity you need to do and evaluating each one's relevance and urgency will help you organize your to-do list.

For instance, some activities may be more essential or urgent than others if they are time-sensitive or have a significant influence on your job or goals.

Once you have determined which chores are most crucial, you may concentrate on finishing them before moving on to other, less vital duties. This might assist you in avoiding squandering time and effort on activities that are unnecessary or can wait till later.

You may manage your workload more effectively, experience less stress and worry, and make sure you are moving closer to your objectives by using effective prioritizing.

2. **Cut disruptions out**.

The best strategy to minimize multitasking is to eliminate distractions because this is one of the primary causes of frequent task switching, which decreases productivity and raises stress levels.

Distractions can take many different forms, including phone or computer notifications, sounds, other people, or even your own thoughts.

**Strong Methods for Eliminating Distractions**

Here are some effective strategies for avoiding and getting rid of distractions:

- **Disable alerts.**

If you want to avoid distractions while working, turn off the alerts on your computer or phone or utilize the "Do Not Disturb" option.

- **Close any unneeded windows and tabs.**

On your computer, keep only the relevant tabs and windows open to prevent being sidetracked by other websites or programs.

- **Utilize headphones with noise cancellation.**

To drown out any distracting sounds around you, put on some noise-canceling headphones or turn on some white noise.

- **Locate a peaceful work area.**

Find a place to work that is peaceful so that you can focus on your job without being disturbed by others or other activities.

- **Establish limits.**

Tell them you are working on something important and urge them to refrain from interrupting you unless it's an emergency.

By eliminating distractions, you can establish a space that enables you to concentrate on one task at a time, which can improve your productivity, lower your stress levels, and assist you in reaching your goals more quickly."

3. **Identification Goals and Due Date.**

By focusing on the most crucial activities and avoiding distractions, setting clear goals might help you avoid multitasking.

How setting goals can benefit you

Here are some strategies for avoiding multitasking that include setting goals:

- **Explicitly states priorities**.

Setting objectives generally involves deciding which activities are most crucial to you. You may prevent multitasking by concentrating your time and effort on the activities that are most important, thanks to this clarity.

- **Offers a precise course of action**.

Goals give your work a distinct direction. Knowing what you're aiming for makes it simpler to avoid becoming distracted by less important chores.

- **Aids in keeping you organized.**

You may make a strategy to accomplish your goals if you have clear objectives. This aids in keeping you organized and concentrated on the particular duties that will enable you to achieve your objectives.

- **Facilitates improved time management.**

Instead of attempting to balance several activities at once, you may focus on one at a time by creating goals and making a timetable for yourself. This may result in higher productivity and better time management.

- **Boosts motivation.**

You are more driven to accomplish your goals when they are apparent to you. This drive can keep you on target and prevent you from becoming sidetracked by other obligations.

"Overall, goal-setting is an effective strategy for preventing multitasking. You may stay focused on the most crucial activities and accomplish your goals by setting priorities, offering a clear direction, staying organized, managing your time well, and improving motivation.

**4. Time boundaries.**

A time management strategy known as "time blocking" involves setting aside certain blocks of time for particular jobs or activities.

By concentrating your attention on one activity at a time and finishing it before going on to the next one, this strategy can help you avoid multitasking. "The primary factor is not time. It is the sole factor" To begin using time blocking, list the activities you need to do and make an estimation of how much time each one will require. Then, set up time in your calendar for each task, remembering to do the most crucial ones first. Make sure you schedule breaks to prevent burnout and boost productivity. Avoid distractions when working on a task, such as social media or email notifications, and give that activity your full concentration. Go on to the next job on your agenda when the allotted amount of time for that work has passed. If you complete a job earlier than the allotted time, utilize the additional time to take a break or do another activity.

Breaking up your day into concentrated blocks of time for each task might help you avoid multitasking. You may do jobs more quickly and with fewer interruptions by concentrating on one at a time, which will enhance your productivity and lower your stress levels.

5. **Manufacturing similar tasks**.

Instead of rotating between distinct sorts of work, batching comparable jobs entails gathering tasks that call for the same abilities, resources, or equipment and performing them all at once. By avoiding multitasking, you may increase your productivity and attention.

For instance, if you have numerous emails that need responses, you may batch them together and respond to all of them at once rather than responding to each one as it comes in. Similar to this, you may arrange a certain time to make all of your phone calls at once rather than stopping your job to make them one at a time throughout the day. To achieve a "flow state" where you can perform things more quickly and effectively, you might batch jobs that need similar concentration or resources.

Additionally, switching between projects takes less time and effort, which increases productivity and decreases distraction. You may prioritize and schedule your work more successfully by batching related activities, which can also help you keep organized and manage your time more effectively. Emails, phone calls, paperwork, research, and other duties may all be handled with this method.

6. **Take periodic breaks.**

By enabling you to rest and concentrate your concentration on one task at a time, taking regular breaks can help you avoid multitasking. When you concentrate on a job for a long time, your concentration and focus may start to waver, which can result in multitasking and reduced productivity. You may return to your job with fresh energy and focus by taking regular pauses that give your brain time to relax and recharge.

Staying focused and avoiding distractions might help you be more productive and produce higher-quality work overall.

It's crucial to understand that taking breaks does not entail doing things that are unrelated to your job or that might be distracting, like checking social media or viewing videos. Instead, take advantage of your breaks to rest and recharge with activities like walking, meditation, or eating a nutritious snack. Overall, taking frequent breaks will help you avoid multitasking and increase your attention and productivity, which will ultimately result in better results and less stress.

7. **Practice being mindful**.

Being mindful means being totally present and involved in the present moment without passing judgment. By assisting you in maintaining your attention on the current task, practicing mindfulness can help you prevent multitasking.

Start your mindfulness exercises by taking a few deep breaths and focusing on your breath. Take note of how your breath feels as it enters and exits your body. If your thoughts begin to stray, gently refocus them on your breathing.

After that, focus on the project you're working on. Take note of the task's specifics, including the colors, noises, and textures. Pay attention to your ideas and feelings as they come up, but try not to label them or let them control you. Bring your focus back to the subject at hand if you find yourself being sidetracked by other projects or ideas. It's important to keep in mind that the aim of mindfulness is to increase awareness of distractions and ideas while also learning to refocus your attention. Being aware can help you stay focused on one job at a time and resist the urge to multitask if you practice it enough.

# Chapter 5

# Developing Mindfulness for Deep Thinking

Finding moments of peace and developing resilience have become very important factors that help us maintain balance, manage stress, and preserve our overall well-being in today's busy world. Staying mindful is a practice rooted in ancient traditions and has gained widespread acceptance as a potent tool for navigating the challenges of daily life.

**Describe mindfulness?**

When we intentionally direct our attention to the present moment, we can better understand ourselves and the world around us. At its core, it is the practice of being fully present and aware of our thoughts, emotions, and physical sensations in the present moment without judgment. It involves cultivating a non-judgmental attitude and a curious, accepting mindset toward our experiences.

**Here are some strategies for using mindfulness to manage stress in our daily lives:**

- **Finding inner calm in the face of chaos**.
Through easy practices like focused breathing, body scans, and mindful meditation, we can cultivate a sense of calmness that permeates our daily lives, enabling us to navigate challenges with greater clarity and composure.
- **Increasing emotional health and resilience**.
Awareness of our thoughts and emotions can better equip us to respond to challenges (acting with greater self-compassion and self-awareness instead of reacting as triggered by how we feel in the moment).
- **Increasing concentration and productivity**.
The human mind is exposed to over 90,000 marketing signals daily, and that's just marketing, which means that our minds are constantly overloaded with information, the

majority of which we don't care about. Remaining mindful can help us focus more clearly and increase productivity by training our attention.

- **Building empathy and relationships**. People who have developed mindfulness are better able to listen intently, communicate clearly, and be fully present with others. Mindful presence allows us to connect more deeply, fostering empathy, understanding, and compassion. By being aware of our own emotions and thoughts, we can better understand the experiences of others, resulting in more meaningful and fulfilling relationships.

## How to develop mindfulness for in-depth contemplation.

Because of its benefits for the mind, body, and soul. Meditation is a potent tool that may help shift our ideas, feelings, and neurological patterns. Practicing mindfulness as much as possible does wonders for our mental health.

How do you cultivate mindfulness? It takes practice; becoming aware is not something that happens suddenly but rather requires years of daily commitment, effort, and patience.

So that you can develop into your most conscious self, this piece will specifically describe that.

- **In-Body Scan.**

This is just about checking in with your body and going through it, so it doesn't have to be a slow practice. Practice scanning your body for a minute, starting with the bottom of your body: your toes, feet, and ankles. Move up through the body and intentionally check each portion until you reach your head.

- **Add in some mindfulness time.**

If you have a minute to spare, put your phone down and just breathe. Be in the moment and experience the present. What can you feel? Examine these moments and sensations for a minute.

- **Recognize your thoughts and feelings**.

We experience a wide range of emotions on a daily basis, including sadness, happiness, anger, and confusion. The next time you react to an event or trigger, consider why you're feeling those emotions and whether there might be another way to think about it. We comprehend that our emotions are merely a reflection of what we are now experiencing once we become aware that we don't need to be as reactive as we believe we need to be.

- **Feel things intentionally**.

Being mindful means paying attention to the here and now and feeling the thoughts, senses, and emotions that are happening all around you, from the wind blowing by to the leaves cracking.

- **Keep an eye on your breathing**.

If you breathe differently, does it feel different? Does it change when you're peaceful? Does it change when you're unhappy, furious, or frustrated? How do you calm yourself using your breath? Do you have a specific technique?

- **Consciousness training**.

It takes time and effort to develop awareness, and the particular mindfulness meditation will really assist you in getting there. This is one of the most well-liked, oldest, and most well-known types of meditation. It entails utilizing your breath to create a relaxing anchor, which in turn helps you focus while reducing tension and anxiety. It also involves meditating while focusing on the moment-to-moment awareness of what is happening in that current moment.

- **Employ the reflect orb**.

In order to help you learn how to manage your daily stress, the Reflect Orb is a biofeedback meditation tool that monitors your physiological signals and reflects them back to you. The Orb and the Reflect App are synchronized, enhancing your experience with information and insights while improving your comprehension of your unique path to relaxation and wellbeing.

It takes years of consistent practice to cultivate mindfulness, so it won't happen overnight. However, once you do, mindfulness will become a way of life for you.

# Chapter 6.

# Useful Techniques for Getting Your Focus Back.

Keep in mind that keeping and recovering attention is a continuous effort. Try out several variations of these methods to see which suits you the most, then tweak your strategy as necessary. You may improve your attention and productivity in several areas of your life over time.

- **Embrace the outdoors.**

 Finding time to take a walk in the park or enjoy the plants or flowers in your garden can boost your concentration and help you feel refreshed. Research has shown that even having plants in office spaces can help increase concentration and productivity, as well as workplace satisfaction and better air quality.

- **Develop your brain.**

Brain training games for concentration can also help you develop your working and short-term memory, as well as your processing and problem-solving skills. Examples of such games include jigsaw puzzles, sudoku, chess, and brain-stimulating video games. Scientific research is beginning to amass evidence on the ability of brain training activities to enhance cognitive abilities, including concentration, in adults.

- **Take a brief rest.**

The ability to focus on anything for a prolonged period of time may start to wane, and you may experience increasing difficulties focusing on the activity at hand. The next time you are working on a project, take a break when you begin to feel stuck. Move around, talk to someone, or even switch to a different type of task. You will come back with a more focused mind to keep your performance high. Researchers have found that our brains tend to ignore sources of constant stimulation. Taking very small breaks by refocusing your attention elsewhere can dramatically improve mental concentration after that.

- **Decide to concentrate on the now.**

While it isn't always easy, make an effort to let go of past events, acknowledge the impact, what you felt, and what you learned from them, and then let them go. Similarly, acknowledge your concerns about the future, consider how you are experiencing that anxiety in your body, and then let it go. It may seem counterintuitive when you feel unable to concentrate, but remember that you choose where you focus.

- **Take more naps.**

Read from a computer, phone, or tablet, or watch your favorite movie or TV show on an LED TV just before bedtime. Research has shown that such devices emit light towards the blue end of the spectrum, which will stimulate your eye retina and prevent the secretion of melatonin that promotes sleep anticipation in the brain. Use a filter or "blue light" glasses to minimize such blue light emissions.

- **Exercise meditation and awareness.**

With practice, we can learn to use our breath to bring our attention back to a specific task so that it can be done well even if we get interrupted. Meditating or engaging in mindfulness activities can strengthen wellbeing, mental fitness, and focus. During the meditation process, our brain becomes calmer and our whole body becomes more relaxed.

- **Limit your multitasking**.

Multitasking, which includes listening to a podcast while responding to an email or talking on the phone while writing a report, not only impairs your ability to concentrate but also lowers the quality of your work. While trying to multitask makes us feel productive, it's also a recipe for lower focus, poor concentration, and lower productivity, which can lead to burnout.

- **Avoid becoming distracted.**

Make a habit of designating time in your calendar for a certain work or activity. During this time, request that you be left alone or travel to a location where others are unlikely to interrupt you: a library, a coffee shop, or a private room.

As reported in HBR, researchers found that cognitive capacity was significantly better when the phone was out of sight, not just turned off. Your primary focus is to complete what you need to do. Shutting off both internal and external disturbances can help you concentrate. Close social media and other apps, silence notifications, and keep your phone hidden from sight in a bag or backpack.

- **Exercise**.

Get your body moving and get it going in the morning. According to the Harvard Men's Health Watch May 2013 edition, daily exercise produces chemicals crucial for memory.

Exercise can increase brain dopamine, norepinephrine, and serotonin levels, which all affect focus and attention. People who engage in some form of physical activity or sports perform better on cognitive tasks when compared to those who are in poor physical health. Physical movement helps relax the muscles and relieve tension in the body. Since the body and mind are so closely linked, when your body feels good, you feel good.

- **Listen to music**.

It has been shown to have therapeutic effects on the brain. Light music may help you concentrate better, but some music may distract you. Experts generally agree that classical music and nature sounds, such as water flowing, are good choices for concentration, while music with lyrics and human voices may be distracting. Several apps and services offer background music and soundscapes designed for various types of focus and work needs.

- **Eat healthy meals**.

Limit sugary foods and beverages that create spikes and dips in your blood sugar levels and make you feel lightheaded or sleepy, and choose foods that moderate blood sugar, sustain energy, and feed the brain. It has been discovered that foods like blueberries can boost concentration and memory for up to 5 hours after consumption due to an enzyme that stimulates the flow of oxygen and blood to the brain, helping with memory as well as our ability to focus and learn new information. Nuts, berries, avocados, and coconut oil are all great ways to get healthy fats into your diet and help your brain run more smoothly. Break large tasks into smaller bytes so that you won't feel overwhelmed. Write down what you want to accomplish each day, ideally the night before, and identify a single priority that you commit to completing. This will help you focus your brain on what matters, tackling the big jobs first and leaving the small stuff till later. Clear clutter out of sight, make it as ergonomic and comfortable as possible, and try to keep your space neat and ventilated. Create a space for work. Create a calm, dedicated space for work, if possible. Not everyone can have a well-appointed office, but desk organizers, noise-canceling headphones, an adjustable monitor, and adjustable lighting can help. Use a timer or phone alarm to train your brain to hyper-focus on a task. First, decide what task you want to complete. Set your timer for 20 minutes (generally not more than 30 minutes). Concentrate on the task. When the alarm rings, take a short break for 5 minutes. You can either go for a walk or do some stretching exercises. Then, reset the timer and start again. Try moving on to other projects or anything you enjoy doing. While we may want to focus on a certain activity, sometimes we become stuck, and our brain needs something else to focus on. Moving tasks may help you stay awake and productive for a longer period of time.

# CONCLUSION

Finally, "Getting Back Your Focus" is more than simply a book; it's a journey toward regaining clarity, control, and purpose in a world full of distractions. You have the ability to not only regain your lost focus but also to completely change your life thanks to the ideas, tactics, and exercises given inside these pages. Keep in mind that you possess the ability to focus, just waiting to be unlocked and applied to achieving your aspirations and goals. You'll discover that restoring your concentration is not only doable but also profoundly satisfying when you put the ideas covered in this book into practice. You are reclaiming an essential piece of your humanity and accepting the boundless possibilities of your intellect with each step you take down this path to increased awareness. So, go ahead with assurance, cultivate your capacity for concentration, and watch as it gives you the capability to do the remarkable in whatever you do.